South of North: Images of Canada

354

SOUTH *of* NORTH
IMAGES OF CANADA

Richard Outram

with drawings by Thoreau MacDonald

selected by Anne Corkett and Rosemary Kilbourn

The Porcupine's Quill

Library and Archives Canada Cataloguing in Publication

Outram, Richard, 1930–2005
    South of north: images of Canada / by Richard Outram;
    selected by Anne Corkett and Rosemary Kilbourn;
    with drawings by Thoreau MacDonald.

Poems.
ISBN 978-0-88984-298-4

    I. Corkett, Anne, 1944– . II. Kilbourn, Rosemary.
    III. MacDonald, Thoreau, 1901–1989. IV. Title.

PS8529.U8S68 2007   C811'.54   C2007-904139-6

Published by The Porcupine's Quill, 68 Main St, Erin, Ontario NOB 1TO.
http://www.sentex.net/˜pql

Represented in Canada by the Literary Press Group.
Trade orders are available from University of Toronto Press.

We acknowledge the support of the Ontario Arts Council and the Canada
Council for the Arts for our publishing program. The financial support of
the Government of Canada through the Book Publishing Industry
Development Program is also gratefully acknowledged. Thanks, also, to
the Government of Ontario through the Ontario Media Development
Corporation's Ontario Book Initiative.

ONTARIO ARTS COUNCIL
CONSEIL DES ARTS DE L'ONTARIO

Canada Council   Conseil des Arts
for the Arts   du Canada

AUGUSTANA LIBRARY
UNIVERSITY OF ALBERTA

Introduction

A year before his death on January 21, 2005, Richard Outram gave each of us a manuscript of 115 unpublished poems entitled *South of North: Images of Canada*. Although titled, the collection was in no particular order. The poems were written in three months in response to a request from the Arts and Letters Club of Toronto to provide a text for a song cycle commissioned from the composer Srul Irving Glick, in celebration of the Club's ninetieth anniversary in 1998. Of the 54 poems presented to him, Glick chose eight,* setting them for baritone/mezzo-soprano and piano. The songs were performed entitled *South of North: In Honour of Thoreau MacDonald 1901–1989*.

Thoreau MacDonald was the son of the Group of Seven's J.E.H. MacDonald, a member of the Arts and Letters Club. Richard had long admired Thoreau's work, maintaining he was the finest graphic artist of them all. He insisted simplicity and restraint are among the most difficult achievements of art. Thoreau agreed, writing of his work, 'These pictures are attempts to show the Harmony and Design of Nature in a small space … as a picture is so limited it is best to eliminate the unnecessary and accentuate the essentials … they represent more the spirit and feeling of the place and time than outer appearance.'

Thoreau's spare, evocative pictures drew from Richard a different aspect of his mastery. The poems are quick, vividly immediate, instant of access. They are the visible, audible delights of a consummate poet's recognition of an artist as passionately involved with animals, country and the right, practical accomplishment of tasks as he was. Both men were deeply grieved by the despoliation of this world.

Unable to sort and arrange the poems and choose illustrations to make a coherent manuscript, Richard had many conversations

---

* The eight poems selected for Srul Irving Glick's performance were: *Wilderness on Centre Island, Vane, Grace, Northern River Falls, Privity, Stripe, Congregation at the Shoreline* and *Windmill*.

with us about its possibilities. He lived to see a preliminary draft we assembled. We chose these poems close to the spirit of Thoreau's pictures by season, vocation and place. Richard's was the guiding hand that placed poems beside those pictures which were their direct inspirations.

The last poem was chosen, not for an obvious relation to any illustration, but for its quiet, profound melding, in nursery rhyme, of Babylon, that destroyed cradle of civilization, with Canada. It lies on the page as a dignified statement and warning of the extent of the loss occurring around us. 'Unless the prevailing misrule is corrected' ... 'a heritage loved and inhabited as such' will be gone. We will not find it again. 'Not before dark.'

May this small book preserve some of the loves of artist and poet. And some of ours.

> — *Anne Corkett & Rosemary Kilbourn*
> The Dingle, Caledon, March 2007

South of North

In honour of Thoreau MacDonald

(1901–1989)

'Helping Mr Jim Pearson plant spuds. A fine evening light on barn and lilacs. Team, barn and light seem of the past, also Jim himself. When they are gone there'll be no trace of that quiet old way of life and when I go, no memory of it even. So I tried to make some drawings of it though writing would be better if it could be done.' (TM., *Journal*, 28 May 1946)

Vane

The copper cock atop
the weathered barn burns
in the first morning's sun,
in the last slant light;

swivels daylong to flourish
aloft viridian plumes,
to brandish his rust crest
in the blazed eye, defiant;

spins with the swift winds
to whet the four quarters
of his whole gold-spurred
world blooded below.

Spring in Algonquin

At last! Look!
The ice is out!
Even fleet light
heels as March wind
cuts white chop
on black water.

Farm Wife

In all of the springtime bustle she would see
small bones of voles whitened under the grass,
the constant rose-auroras of swamp osiers,
flared in drifts still hidden in cedar-darkness.

Fingerling

Ice spring
cold creek
flow cuts
cress green
light look
dart quick
brook trout!

Late April, Near Newcastle

A wake of white gulls rises behind the red tractor,
settles, screaming, back on the wet black furrows.

Someone has painted the pump on the side porch
green-apple green; and the tin dipper is blaze.

Spring light kindles the scarlet geranium on the sill
of the kitchen window, creaks on the washed glass.

There is water running in ditches and bright sheets
on the steaming fields riffle the huge blue day.

Winds gust in the orchard, spoil in the roseate haze
of quick buds thrust up to the cockerel sun.

Shining April Morning

Old snow, grainy, deep in the swale,
pointing the terra-cotta dogwoods,
the clumped cinnabar-green alders;

and snow left in the curved furrows,
leaving the sloped field ribbed with
black welts, brilliant with wet glint;

water-trickle everywhere, the day
polished in thin spring light. Crows,
raucous, slant into the sun's dazzle.

Shock in the High Arctic

When two
brute rut-
clenched
musk ox
herd bulls
charge,

smash
seismic
granite
boulder
skulls
together,

glaciers
hard by
calve.

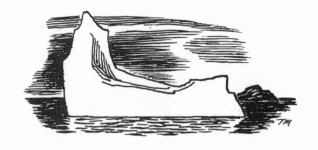

The Horses of Bonavista

The horses of Bonavista pick their deliberate, delicate way
between sprawled stonepiles, graze between stone shelves.

Scrawny, shaggy, still dazed by the thin spring sunshine,
they ignore the elaborate, massive icebergs passing offshore.

The drifting crags, the lofted dazzle of antique ice, are common:
a great, green, summerspread maple might well spook them.

May in the Caledon Hills

Stepping a moment into the soft night,
last thing before bed, dazzled at first
from lamplight still bright on the page;

and the pulsed relentless deafening throb
of frog sound swelled from the black pond
makes even the nearby green stars quiver.

Wilderness on Centre Island

As rain white-pocks the olive water
of the lagoon, under flailed willows
a small flock of Canada geese roots,
probes, softly complaining, across
the cropped, mortal emerald grass.

Weathered Cabin Back of Beyond

There were hard births and deaths in this single room
at the foot of the sheltering esker. The unsquared logs
were chinked with caribou moss. Up in the plank loft,
where the heat rose, in winter the honeybucket froze.

Now the rank lilac is grown to crumbled chimney height;
someone lugged out what was left of the stove for scrap;
the precious, flawed glass of the window is long broken.
In this midsummer meadow, however, it floats on light.

Storm Cellar

The slanted, weathered, board-and-batten doors,
back of the summer kitchen, was the ideal place
to stretch out, soaking up the first gold April sun
behind rose-fired eyelids closed on perfect worlds.

While it is understood, if seldom mentioned, how
nowadays the doors are kept fast padlocked lest
raged blackness pent, come boiling forth before
our very eyes, obliterate this endless gentian day.

Privity

O sweet sweet
flame oriole,
inflecting the light
of green summer
over and over.

Stunted, ragged,
the hedgerow crosses
threadbare pasture,
with scrub, cream-
blossomed hawthorn
entangled in pitted
lichen-mottled
rocks and skulls.

Across the field,
a stand of black
motionless ash
cast extended
diagonal shadow
under the summoned
name-graven white
stone moon.

Tantramar Marsh

Under these billowed silver enormous heavens
the world is that level forever and then landfall,
a stranger might perish over the elm-lashed edge.

The winds that buffet the sunset-blood-roofed barns,
scattered like squared glacier tailings across a barrens,
can stagger us breathless, promise us stayed flight.

The long beautiful dirt roads run straight as truth,
right out of a man's sight: the glitter of water fired
in a narrow ditch is blessing and brief bright death.

A Grace Note in June

Is, in a grazed pasture, the given
space between single maples,
abundant above cow level;

or between the hazed fountains
of elms in rockpiled fence lines,
each of its own green flourish.

Summer Storm in Cobourg

Like a root beer float with the amber clouds run right overhead
and the Lombardy poplars backlashing their muslin underleaves
in the sideways white rain and the little kids cavorting about
in the frothed gutters naked and the dog hiding under the bed;

and sheet lightning fried the day bluegreenblue again and again
and the sidewalks smelled of hot-sun-wet-electric-cement smell
and you couldn't hear your own voice cracking shouting and then
it was all over, with everything left stunned, drenched, dripping.

Praise of Fishes

Who has seen,
and not admired,

perch threading
green streamers,

sunfish fanning
gravel shallows,

trout rising
into evening,

carp glinting
pewter greaves,

dying salmon
leaping rapids,

bass basking
next to lilies,

shiners flashing
veered fire,

and the breeding
rainbow darter?

Morning on South Bay

As starveling wraiths of mist diminish,
and intimations of the winds begin
to quicken poplars, an entangled sun
spills across the restless darkness
in splintered light where burnished
waves, flame-burdened, break.

Muskeg

Close to the low bog-scrubbed edge
of one of countless nameless lakes,
a rigid great blue heron glares
past its own hunched image down
through the mirrored forever sun
into the clear copper-tinted water.

After another forever it takes
a single, slowly unfolded step.

Brightness

Having survived the nightlong
lances of ancient starlight,
the batter of velvet moths,
woven between the veranda's
elaborate zinc gingerbread
and the pale lilac, the ragged
orb-web at first morning
has captive for one immortal
instant the trembled theorems
of water-beads, the sun's
slant white rage.

Saugeen River

Has muscled gasping cold out of the cedar bush
summer and winter, curved steady as gospel
across the south forty since anyone recollects.
It was where, certain from childhood, the hymn
invited us all to gather. To slake our thirst, five
generations: 'for they shall be filled'. Her mother
never but brightened when she recalled it, lost
in her cot in the Home. You didn't think twice,
to drink of it then from cupped palms, kneeling
work-stunned under the shuddered noonday sun,
dripping His living silver between your fingers
back into His shining everlasting glory. Nowadays
only God and the government could say, maybe,
whatever darkness gets dumped into it upstream.

Dark Walden Song

Night like contagion spreads
out over the furrowed fields;
the moon won't rise till dawn.
At last, the whippoorwill
has done with its quivered rote,
that drove the one point home:
night like contagion spreads.

Main Line near Bowmanville

Premonition troubles the stone roadbed;
crashed steel slams past promise of
canyon, muskeg, grassland, spruce bog,
the ocean margins of flashing distance.

Rotted baulks of hemlock left stacked
at the base of the timber trestle harbour
copper centipedes, white-lipped snails,
a salamander wrapped in chill fox-fire.

Barred Owl

Old eight-hooter:
over and over on still
midsummer nights
freezes small hearts,

as a stone-blind moon
stares white shadow
across black pastures.

Stripe

In great
shrill fuss
the chip-
munk on
the cedar
stump was
there is
here has
now raced
along the
rail fence
halts atop
a mossed
boulder
to scold
poor un-
striped un-
tailed un-
gainly in-
trusive
mere
us!

July

What a tremendous clatter and racket of hard green light
spilled down from leaf to leaf through the maple's crown,
and look at the turquoise arabesques, the molten bronze
wires of birdsong criss-crossing this buckwheat morning,
at the coarse homespun of silver-smouldered daybreak.

Dawn

Blinds still down: but thin blue smoke
arrows up from the farmhouse.

Swiftly ribbed light climbs, feral,
up and over the furrowed drumlin.

Beyond the cedars a dog fox coughs. Once.
An axe-blow cracks daybreak.

Childbed

Barely two square rods; still fenced with rusted wire;
set back upon a rise. Enclosed, three sides, with corn
gone parchment sere, head-height, like vertical dry fire.

Each car that passes drags behind a billowed cloud
of hovered, sallow dust, this season of the year,
that drifting in the heat, sifts ash-fine down to shroud

the frost-heaved monuments. One purple granite stone
seems set a piece apart, surrounded as it is
by small, white stones laid flat, now mostly overgrown.

It marks a husbandman, who earned a local fame
for Christian rectitude; his three beloved wives.
And he outlived them all. His common Scottish name

and dates are legible; some others weathered dim.
One can make out his third, brief, almost child bride wife.
Beneath her name is carved, 'I shall go to him.'

Late August

Heat like a giant hand
flattens the mown field,
shimmers bronze furrows:

over the sere stubble, hung
in the sun's one eye,
a kestrel hovers.

Attendant in Manitoba

With a terrible steel screech the buzz-saw sun
rips through the blazing July mid-afternoon.

The old collie dog, flat as a pelt in the shifting
lilac shade of the shed, being dreamed, twitches.

The calico cat tucked on the granite sill ignores
all the ruckus; she has tasks of greater moment

to be getting on with: the constant, meticulous
grooming of fleet light, all the while watching

the crazed gyrations of hatches of bright motes
intent on getting the vivid better of one another.

Solitary

His sunflowers arched parlous against
the weathered board-and-batten south
side of the old house. Year after year.

Cloud shadow raced over ripe wheat
in the sun-drenched, sloped far field
could remove him beyond measure.

And the sudden unmuffled rumble
of winter thunder sometimes heard
in the white gloom of a snowstorm.

He'd stand forever as if distracted,
watching the old marmalade tom
washing in brittle spring sunlight.

Elder Remembering

Out on the west veranda, watching
the last of the sunset, bloody beyond
the boundary hedgerow, descending.

They went, gone in his time, we are all
altered forever, never again to remark
fulfilled the green summer upwelling.

A loss beyond sadness, acceptance:
now, only rarely, in ashen dreams
can he fathom his childhood elms.

Scrub Country

Sometimes, winding along the back dirt roads
with no poles, with snake fences straggled now
and again; concession lines where the corduroy
heaves each spring in the low swamp stretches,

you can glance down a deep, wavering, narrow
lane and catch, at dusk, a single, small, orange-
yellow, distant, low to the ground window, still
lit by a coal oil lamp's soft light within. Home.

Near Queensborough

This ledged and shelved limestone
and juniper scrub landscape is left
fenceless, unpastured, for miles on end;
it has yet to recover from man's first
lumbering, several generations past,
when the last of the pine went.

Here scant crops wither, parched
over countless underground rivers
branched endlessly out of sight.

Where mullein spikes poked straight
at the noon day from scoured stone
in a season reach to a man's height,
lichens, with all the time in the world,
continue to spread their intricate rings
from a vanished original centre out
to the rumoured ends of the earth.

Snapping Turtle

This dripping, green-slime-fringed, domed stone
has heaved its matte black bulk, trailing a rank
ooze of bottom muck up onto a granite outcrop.
Its thrust, leeched neck like a wrist-thick, beaked
phallus is bent erect to the throbbed noon sun.
Its black claws curled on its splayed webbed feet
are needled hooks. Its ridged tail is limp, uncurled.
Its smouldered, mottle-lidded, small bulged eyes
are clamped shut. Cold-veined, its plated carapace
baked, its hidden, augured plastron dank, it basks
immobile, rock on rock. A haze of iridescent flies
is busy about its leather bellows flanks. A brute
creature enacted: a former eon's battered survivor.

'That cuts the airy way'

It is difficult to think
of a great horned owl,
perched unruffled
and bolt upright
in the dark heart of
the dense hemlock,
hidden from crows,
stinking to high heaven
of fresh skunk,
its amber occasional
swivelled sniper's
levelled scrutiny
raking the swamp's
luminous gloom,
as an 'immense world of delight':

but what do we know?

Nightfall

Perched either side of the amethyst glass knurl,
swallows chitter and preen, black specks against
the enormous inflamed mother-of-pearl evening,

on a single black wire strung from one tilted pole
to the next, diminishing swiftly over the darkened,
featureless, uninhabited grassland as if forever.

Inflection and Innuendo

This boat-tailed grackle in actual fact, back-
lit in the leafless ash is black, soot-black, jet black
against soft evening's lofted, luminous pearl surround.

The grackle remembered, fired in full sun preens
noon-sleek plumage of glazed, of oil-rose sheens,
anthracite gloss of gunmetal blues, rare bottle-greens.

Abandoned Orchard

In mortal summer do not look up
lest diamond fire lanced down
pierces the green greaves,
blinds you forever.

In barren winter do not cast down
your gaze lest crystal dazzle
forever reflected scar
your mortal sight.

In springtime's blizzard cream-wreath
blossom woven, lashed about you,
writhe, by long-forgotten gods
watched, immortal.

With autumn's mortal abundance hung
for the gold grasping before you,
with russet suns strewn
at your feet, weep.

Farmhouse Kitchen Window

It is night on the dark hillside; beyond,
rare starlight falls into the black ocean
of never forever. But the coal oil lamp
on the cleared table rings homework
of pecks and rods and bushels and chains
and legends of grammars that sometime
encircle even the lost wilderness, kindled
above the wood stove, for ever and ever.

Nowadays

You're still peckish, you eat the whole store-bought loaf.
It was about the only winter anyone ever remembered
when metal got stone-brittle, and the south well froze.

At the back of our nickel-skirted Northland wood stove,
in the blue granite-ware basin, covered over with a red
and green checked clean apron, always, her bread rose.

Rural Wisdom

All barn cats,
they sound alike
as an Antigonish
or a Yellowknife
election speech.

All barn cats,
they thrive alike
as a Drumheller
or a Sept Isles
car salesman.

All barn cats,
they look alike
in a Saskatchewan
or a Cape Breton
winter whiteout.

Citified cats,
they sure are
a whole other
proposition
altogether.

Questions of Barns

But what of abandoned barns?

With heaved sills, sagged doors,
split tenons and skewed beams,
with nettles and burdock rank
on collapsed cribbed ramps?

With the gnawed stalls vacant?

What of the swift birdflight
in one side and out the other?

What of the long darkness
gathered within them on
late summer afternoons,
and the darkness without?

Landmark

For no discernible reason, three generations have chosen
to plough round this basswood. Its heart-shaped leaves
are as broad as a man's hand. Its trunk is long hollowed.
Its parchment samaras are spinning through burnished
September lightfall, down to the spinning earth. Briefly.

Autumn

And some diminished days a grave man's mind
drifts, from the hazed horizon on to a vivid other,
passes like vast patterns of cumulus cloud thrown
across the long reaches of tawny prairie, quilting
grassland with scattered blaze, with cast shadow.

Late October, near Lakefield

Mad colour gone
from the Kawarthas;
the mornings hoar;

and a late haze,
a spiralled hatch
of frenzied motes
spins in sudden
noonday sun,
smokes over
rose granite:

Indian summer
in bronze autumn.

Congregation at the Shoreline

The water is mortal,
all perturbation
of flaked fire.

In slow succession,
small waves arrive,
furthering light.

The willows are clustered
with amber flints,
with orange flame:

throughout deep violet
gardens monarchs
hover and pulse.

Maple

In the molten of late autumn
this crimson-ochre billow,
inflamed in the rough gold
field, leaps to the sun's eye.

Balance

In a midnight billow of spectral colours,
of northern auroras welling and fading
and wavering overhead their unearthly
greens and streamers of thinned saffron,
their sudden estranged reds and thrown
curtains of pale mauve, of silvered violet,

the exact, elongated, austere shadow
thrown on the starlit crust, of a cutter
with swanned runners, its tapered shafts
canted back earthwards, out by the old
drive shed, is someone's trued Euclid.

Yukon September

Under the yellow lilies'
viridian pads, the shadowed bass
fan backwards, amazed;

a squirrel, chiding the sun
for shining, curls to a copper knot,
hunched in the white birch;

even the jays are astonished
by sudden intrusion into their blue
spruce wilderness fastness;

on the burnished tawny river,
flowing from some far nowhere
to dark downstream, nothing

so comely has ever been seen
as this green canoe, slicing the silent
current to swerved silver.

Four Augmented Recollections

Morning Mist at Cavendish

The world is all gleamed void, save,
between the honeyed buttocks of two dunes,
a dark blue delta writhes.

October at Stony Lake

In the still, reflected stand
of birch saplings everything,
exact, is black notation and
wavered yellow excellence.

Qualicum River

On a feeder creek threading the mist
through constant moss-green gloom
under the dripping cedar canopy,
every ripple flows emerald velvet.

Long Beach, Vancouver Island, 1950

A glimmered lamp in the single
cedar-shingled shack set back
from crashing darkness throws
gold to the overwhelmed ocean.

Port Hope Garden

On a pewter November morning,
a child finding Tolman Sweets:

flecked yellow windfalls lost
in deep tousles of silvered grass
under the gnarled, lopsided tree
gibbeted from the hillside and

O

rooted in Eden and all suns
remembered forever the first
apples and ever the golden last.

Legend

The side garden in winter resembles nothing
so much as a blank white page with some few
brown squiggles in broken rows. A weightless
fox sifted across it last night, naming nothing
under the moon, but pinking the dusted crust,
just here, just there, on a slant angle that says
almost everything marginal, still left to be said.

November Chores

Fresh snow dusted across the iron furrows;
the hardwood bush black tangle against the sun;
and nothing ever so dazzling since first Eden
as flayed light on the ice, rejoicing the morning.

Hot Stove Talk

You need to have laboured a good few harvest seasons,
forked green hay till you ached deep in your bone-sleep,
to come to understand, maybe, Isaiah's 'all flesh is grass.'

There are no shadows as long as the smoke-
blue snow shadows cast on the crust by a late
December afternoon's cold scapegoat sun.

She could even hear, they said, far underground water;
could name you each horse in the dark barn by its scent;
could watch a mourning dove ascend into white fire.

Farmhouse Bedroom

Midwinter iron
dawn on the hoar
pane tracefires
strictures of Egypt
geometries, frost-
ferns and lianas
of lush jungle.

A woman deftly
combing over
a chipped white
porcelain basin,
watches her gauze
breath in the dark
mirror darken,
vanish.

Love

That strand of barbed wire is threaded deep into the maple;
well, the gnarled trunk has grown through the years around it.
A child who has the lay of the farmland, the untold knowing,
the trued heft of it all, can't say how, won't ever confound it.

Wife

In one of those low, cloud-covered,
moonless evenings,
there is his lantern moving about
after supper,
down by the barn's huge darkness.

In January,
nothing whatsoever under the sun
is brighter.

Recluse

They closed her eyes and lest rude life regard her,
placed a clean apron on her face, in simple state
upon the moss rose oilcloth-covered table lying,

in her cold kitchen, not the frozen peopled parlour.
The road was heavy-drifted and he came too late
to question death, or hinder untoward her dying.

East of Coboconk

Never heard tell of a seasoned maple knot
that a good man couldn't split with a sledge
and a pair of wedges. There's nothing much
burns hotter, embers longer, to powder ash.

Takes the edge off it. She's been gone now
a year. Some spring nights she was quick
as moonlight on river water, as elsewhere.

Midwinter near Sutton

The overnight snowfall has so covered even the cedars,
the entire world on this still morning is black and white.

It is difficult to imagine spring, greening the spare elms;
or wind-moiled, burnished wheat in the blanketed fields;

or the urgent mercury current ever again reflecting high
summer's drifted azures, in the iced reproof of a hidden

river snaked across patchwork farmlands. Yet one must.

Memories of Childhood Winters

His first snowshoes were the bottoms
of six-quart baskets, tied to his shoepacks
with lamp wick. But even without them,
he could scamper over a bearing crust
where his parents would break through,
left floundering behind him.

The taste of caked snow on wet woollen
mittens was never the same in the city.

The seat was kept until spring
leaning behind the wood stove;
you carried it out under your parka.
And remembered to bring it back.
Or else.

Sleep like the night was absolute:
a black owl's soundless
instant descent.

December, Lake Athabaska

The winter stillness, the muffled silence,
the silver lustre of late afternoon light
in the drift-heaped heart of the bush;

they are everywhere, and are not there,
like thick flaked snow steadily descending,
falling on open water.

Prospector

As he is comfortable, she
leaves: and he, remembering
a trembled polestar dawn,
the crazed magenta sunsets,
heads out on whitecapped
cobalt water for the distant
rumoured lodestone islands,
low-lying, darkened, found
far beyond a day's paddle.

Expedition

It seems the fabled northwest passage and
the fabled northeast passage at last meet;

at the arctic centre of starved men's minds
under a white-stunned sun circling the white,

boundless, featureless, white-wired-horizon:
in the absolute cold of a man's absolute death.

Briar Island

The dangerous red
railing and roof
on the white light-
tower with the green
padlocked door
at the very end
of the island chain
keeps us here
steadfast from
stark peril.

Four Moments of Rivers

Yellow shrub willows
clinging to shifting sandbars
in swift-fired shallows.

A sweeping, immense current
rounding the arctic basalt,
nearing the green sea.

Evening light bounced back
from the undergrowth of alders:
blood on black water.

Thirst, thirst in the parched
badlands: a doe, wary,
comes down to drink.

The Sleeping Giant

In the light of all the starlight ever reflected
from Lake Superior back to the black nights
of unwary eyes; and of that noonday flame
snapped from the topmost brightwork of one
freighter steaming just over the far horizon,
deep-laden out of Duluth to deliver iron ore
for eastern smelters, we might never regret

that it will not awaken forever in our time.

Home Port

From far out on the heaved
havenless sea, the two
copper-sheathed spires
receding, maddened
in afternoon light, are
straightforward: death-
tipped arrows aimed at
the wavering heavens.

Morning near Digby

A chill sheen is washed on the muffled foreshore;
curtains of fine white rain sift insistently down
on the shrouded, abruptly vanishing mastheads:
A nearby deliberate ocean crashes, waits, crashes;
the shingle falls back into its seethed death-rattle;
somewhere, here only all opalescent indirection,
the abundant sun will have risen, lethal above us.

String Figures

In Povungnituk, and Masset,
even in midtown Toronto,
it is still, for the time being,
miraculous commonplace:
that a few dextrous persons
can bring to life from a loop
of sinew, realms of legend
shared before or beyond
the telling; and show forth
earth's elements, patterns
of scattering constellations,
the gestures of weather, even
spirits of dreamed creatures;
forms of the fearful kind
to which they are birthright.

Manitoulin Island

Flailing *manomin* into the bark canoe
with her paddle, she freezes and stares
when a beaver ripples past, its curled
wake widening over the frosted inlet.

Having eaten fat beaver; and knowing
how, in some desperate winter, another
barely remembered creature will cross
darkness to girdle the pale dreamtree.

Laurentian Shield Menhir

Where glaciers, withdrawing, have left it,
older than reason, the gold-ochre lichens
that cling to this massive boulder standing,
fired in mica-spangled, immediate sunlight,
reflected wavered however in riffled water,
refine it to infinite grain in adamant season.

Northern River Falls

A curled constant, bulged surge,
bright-underbellied cola slow-
muscled over granite outcrop

>rips through torn
>light a fountain
>down of stained
>lace smashed
>to crashed foam
>on boulders forty
>brutal feet below
>to deafen even
>silence, then

whirlpools, swirls bonecold about
its deepscoured pothole, heaves
white water boiling on between
strewn jagged rocks, abandoning

a knot of otters after flicked trout,
drifts of blazed spray rainbows.

North of Point-No-Point

Mist-wrapped Amphitrite light,
uninhabited now, slashes, howls
at the sea from on high, its back
turned on moiled waves of salal:

still warns the far east, to distant
westward, of present peril.

At the Polynya

Horizoned at midday, Helios haloes
the cast-iron piebald ridges encircling
the inlet. Mottled narwhals blowing,
intent as ever on feeding, leave rare
garlands of vapour trailing, gracing
no virginal damsel, luring no unicorn,
testing the seas for ingenious poison.

Two Mortal Reflections

I

Noon sun on open water

scythewhite scythelight fire
sliced from the bright lake eye
seared blazeback fierce here ...

II

Full moon on black lake

coldest phosphor wavered column
crossing darkness breaching wave
darkness breaking in the inner eye ...

Bay of Fundy Event

In the Minas
Basin's autumn
light countless
migrant sand-
pipers flung
in tight formation
rise and fall,
swerve and veer,
returned as one
bright instant
creature: how,
with neither
hesitation
nor collision,
being something
else we restive
vagrants never
come to under-
stand.

Dipper

Not miraculous, but
amazing: to have seen
this sooty little ousel
breasted with quick-
silver bubbles bustle,
zigzag upstream,

walking underwater
in the iced jade green
shallow torrent of
the boulder-broken
Illecillewaet river,
or the Similkameen.

Grace

In the luminous, pearl, interior day,
on a long, rainswept silver reach
of willow-bordered meadow river,

a pair of sure, fastidious, white
mute swans is drawn, carefully,
thoughtfully, on downstream.

High Foothills, Alberta

This first morning a blond cougar,
drifted from sparse hemlock cover,
skirting the swaths of mauve snow
picks its way through loose scree
across the matted alpine meadow,
stares out over the spruce-shagged
canyon into the sun's white eye.

Of Temperate Mind

There very well may be seductive
burnished islands of mahogany
and umber shadow strewn about
in chartreuse afternoon lagoons;
rare elsewheres, elsewhere: here

a single jagged spruce, ink black against
uncompromising noonday, will suffice
to point on azure field our blazoned sun.

North of Algoma

Caught up in the midwinter pulsed
cold-flared far-flung fire above one,
in nights of night-shifting auroras
of acid-electric-metallic melding
of greens and silvers and sanguines
spun from an absent sun O then

hurled north of north where more
than the eye can follow the blazed
trails of pivoting constellations.

Barrens in Moonlight

Within mid-
winter's rare
absent white
everywhere
for dear life
an arctic hare
present frozen
on pale snow
is not there.

Arctic Myth

When the merciless serpent first sloughed our galaxy, left
its lofted translucent brilliance above us, some say forever,
where, black slithering into blackness then, did it vanish?

Into our coiled darkness: to wind through countless northern
seasons down as forked glaciers calving into amazed oceans;

To lie ice-blooded under the wheeled sun, the barbed starlight:
endless as screamed wind-drift whitesnaked over our barrens.

Coast to Millennial Coast

The waves of Whiffinspit break,
like the waves of Pond Inlet, again
and again at the feet of the poet;
play, slather the shingle, retreat,
in the mind of an azure mariner.

That flash of uncanny fire
far out on the wrinkled horizon
is surely the steadfast sunlight
reflected from someone's glass,
trained on the silent watchers
lining the fractal shoreline:
someone diminishing, leaving;
or someone of stature arriving,
who knows, maybe glad day
after the former tomorrow?

'Threescore miles and ten'

The problem with what most matters,
a heritage loved and inhabited as such,
in Babylon bordered by three tarnished
seas and one more-or-less straight line,
is that all too soon, unless the prevailing
misrule is corrected, one won't be able
to get there from here any longer. Not
before dark.

About the Author

Richard Outram (1930–2005) was born in Oshawa, Ontario. He graduated from the University of Toronto (English and Philosophy) and laboured for many years at the Canadian Broadcasting Corporation as a stagehand crew leader. He wrote more than twenty books, four of which were published by the Porcupine's Quill. Outram won the City of Toronto Book Award in 1999 for his collection *Benedict Abroad* (St Thomas Poetry Series). His poetry is the subject of a book-length study, *'Her kindled shadow…': An Introduction to the Work of Richard Outram*, by Peter Sanger (Nova Scotia: The Antigonish Review, 2001/2002).

Outram married the painter and wood engraver Barbara Howard in 1957. Together they produced many exemplary books and broadsides under their own private press imprint, the Gauntlet Press. In 1999 both poet and artist were celebrated with an exhibition of their many collaborations at the Robarts Library, University of Toronto, and with the publication of a special issue of *The Devil's Artisan: A Journal of the Printing Arts* (Number 44). A cyber-exhibition of Gauntlet Press broadsides entitled Ms Cassie continues to be featured on the Porcupine's Quill web site.

About the Artist

Thoreau MacDonald (1901–1989) was born in Toronto, Ontario. His formative years were spent in rural areas near High Park, and in Thornhill, north of Toronto. Thoreau's drawings and writings about the wild plants and animals native to these regions reflect his deep concern for nature and support for conservation.

Thoreau created thousands of images including pencil sketches, pen and brush drawings, stencils, linocuts, woodcuts, silkscreens, watercolours and oils. He is perhaps best remembered for creating detailed line drawings of natural objects set within their stylized habitats.

Under his Woodchuck Press imprint, Thoreau designed and published sixteen books or booklets of his own work. His drawings and calligraphy have adorned hundreds of books written by others, most notable among which are *Flint and Feather*, E. Pauline Johnson, 1924; *Lyrics of Earth*, Archibald Lampman, 1925; *The Chopping Bee and other Laurentian Stories*, Brother Marie Victorin, 1925; *West by East*, J. E. H. MacDonald, 1933; *Maria Chapdelaine*, Louis Hémon, translated by W. H. Blake, 1938; *Anne of Green Gables*, Lucy Maud Montgomery, 1942; and *David and Other Poems*, Earle Birney, 1942.

Thoreau MacDonald was the son of the Group of Seven member J. E. H. MacDonald. His work is found in the National Gallery of Canada in Ottawa, Hart House at the University of Toronto, the Art Gallery of Ontario, and the McMichael Canadian Art Collection among others.

DUCIT AMOR
PATRIÆ